ECONOMICS FOR INFANTS

WRITTEN BY STEVEN KATES
ILLUSTRATED BY LIAM CAPPELLO

Connor Court Publishing

Published in 2017 by Connor Court Publishing

Connor Court Publishing Pty Ltd
PO Box 7257
Redland Bay QLD 4165
sales@connorcourt.com

www.connorcourt.com

Phone 0497 900 685

ISBN: 978-1-925501-438

Cover design, Liam Cappello

Printed in Australia

To my grandchildren

Matilda, Eve and Louis

You are now at the start of life.

You find the world is just so designed that everything others can think of that will make life good finds its way to you without you having to do a thing.

You are fed. You are bathed. You are given toys and presents. It all just keeps coming and you don't have to do a thing.

Life, you think, couldn't be better.

In fact, it will get better but that is when you have finally grown up.

It is important to understand that things are this way right now only because you are at a very early stage of life.

You have your parents, you see. And there is the rest of the family. And there are your parents' friends.

They all find you adorable and wish to do whatever they can to make your life as good as it could be.

But as good as this is, and as much as you might wish this to go on forever, that is not how it will be.

You must understand that this is how it is right now, not how it will always be.

There will be a time when you get others to give you the things you want, you will have to give them something else in exchange.

And as strange as this may seem, when that time comes, that will be even better than things are now, as much as you like the way things are now.

Most importantly, you must never think of the government in the same way as you now think of your parents.

The government is not there to give you things although they might pretend that this is what they do.

You cannot look to the government to feed you, to give you clothes, to keep you warm, to give you presents.

The government does not even care about you, not even a tiny bit. They don't have any idea who you are or anything else about you.

That is the nature of governments. We no longer live in a village. The world is large and has billions of people.

Only your family and friends know you.
Only they really care about you. To
everyone else you are a stranger.

Others will be mostly polite and nice to you because they are mostly polite and nice to everyone. Just like you are to everyone else.

It may be a bit early to tell you this, but everything that you get – food, clothing, presents – all of these exist only because someone worked very hard to produce them. Someone had to work before they could be given to you.

If they are to give you something, you must give them something back.

Others only give us things because we were able to buy these things with the money we earned ourselves. We earn money by working to produce other things that others can buy.

And one day, if all goes well, you too will produce things for others so that you can buy from them what you want for yourself.

And most interesting of all, as young as you are, if you know and truly understand this, you will know and truly understand something very few adults even understand.

Someone has to produce if you are to buy. And if you are to buy, you will first have to produce.

But that is for the future. Life will
continue to be good and you will seldom
be asked to contribute to producing
food, clothing, toys or any of the other
things you have and enjoy.

One day you will. And when the time comes, you will really want to join in and be part of the working world.

But not now. You are still a baby. You are still the most adorable creature in the world. That time will come, but it has not come yet.

The End

www.ingramcontent.com/pod-product-compliance
Lightning Source LLC
Chambersburg PA
CBHW040856100426
42813CB00015B/2811